Copyright

Disclaimer

These are the tips that have worked for me. If you feel that you might be experiencing challenges that require more significant help, please seek a medical professional.

Introduction

I WANTED TO ADD MY PERSPECTIVE TO THIS TOPIC BECAUSE, IN MY LIFE, I HAVE EXPERIENCED A SPECTRUM OF BREAKUPS. WHICH INCLUDED TOXIC, LONG-SUFFERING, AND SOME EERILY LONG-STANDING REACTIONS FROM EXES WHO DIDN'T ACCEPT THE RELATIONSHIP'S ENDING. WHY DID IT EVEN CONTINUE, YOU MIGHT ASK?
WE'LL GET TO IT LATER ON.

Jokingly, some people would say that I did something "good." Still, there was nothing good about having to repeat the same thing several times. It also made things weird if I felt cornered to say it more powerfully, which has led some like me to look over their shoulder and feel unsafe. But not all breakups result in these situations.

Pain is universal; you are unique.

You might be the type that secretly still feels pain and can't let go no matter how hard you might try. I'm here to say it's not too late to heal and offer support and some hard truths with doable solutions that will help you move on like a boss.

Having to worry about ending a relationship after a relationship has ended should be something that no one should have to deal with at any time. Especially when it is severely unwanted, and the person has said it is over.

Is this book for me?

This book is not about bashing anyone or assuming that all of these instances happened or were entirely on you. It's not about saying that you are a sick, twisted, psychotic cheater or bully that won't let go!

Understandably, some questionable actions have earned you some of those impressions, and I'm here to say that you don't have to be that person or thought of as one.

So how did we get here?

For a plethora of reasons to choose from, the end result was parting ways. We have what I like to call the 10 triggers that cause a breakup. I will discuss how they all play intricate parts in a connection's finality in the following pages.

In the end, you will receive tips on how to turn the tables in your life to better yourself and boss up to your highest potential.

These tips are not about winning someone back, although they might help others if they choose to do so. The purpose of these points is to give you a blueprint of what usually happens to cause the downfall and what you can do to pick yourself back up and keep it moving forward.

You don't have to live in a world where people see you strangely based on someone's experience with you. Nor do you have to see yourself strangely if someone no longer wants to be with you. You have the power to change your circumstances for the better.

However, you cannot control how others, including your ex, see you. Even if you decide to skip everything in this book and try to win your ex's heart back (who doesn't want you), I can guarantee this, it will never be the same, and you will keep chasing something that you didn't allow to be set free nor the free-will to return on its own

Remember, this is not about pointing fingers; it's about getting to the pain, healing, and moving forward. Before we can win again, we have to playback the scenes, figure out what went wrong, and then learn from it and heal like a boss.

Are **YOU** ready?

Let's get started.

1. Jealousy

Jealousy has its pros and cons. Everyone wants to feel wanted, desired, and have their significant other's eyes stuck on them only. It gets toxic when you take it overboard and turn that jealousy into a "we problem" and start blaming your partner for your reactions. Don't get me wrong, there are two sides to a story, and then there is the situation's truth.

Let's say your partner was faithful for argument's sake but was very friendly. How did one of their attractive traits turn into a problem? Let's say there have been no behavioral changes, but all of a sudden, you see the waiter is too friendly with them. The likes on Instagram are too much, and the possibility of them taking it to the next level increases by the second.

At this point, in your mind, anything is possible. This incident reminded you of a past relationship. Or, it was you who was the friendly, popular one back then. Now the tables have turned, and you are struggling to handle it. In this case, how can they possibly win?

Your judgment is becoming more clouded, and you are not taking responsibility for affecting your relationship. The shift is now taking place, and the signs of your fears are starting to seep through. You might say that it's not too bad; you can apologize, give a gift, be sweeter, show more affection, and stop what you're doing for about two weeks.

BUT TRUST ME WHEN I TELL YOU WHEN YOU GIVE YOUR WORD OF AN APOLOGY, AND THEN YOU BACKPEDAL, IT WILL ONLY GET WORSE.

2. Cheating

No one likes to be deceived and have their heart, mind, or body played with in any way. What does cheating mean to you? I ask because some people have different meanings or standards for something to be considered offensive. Is it sleeping with someone else? Or, is it kissing or having an emotional connection?

Is it sliding into someone's DM's? Is it creating a dating profile?

I get it. Not to make an excuse for it, but sometimes you are at a crossroads with a relationship, and - things happen.

Or, everything was okay but not that great. Let's say you got caught, and all hell breaks loose, and now you have a come to Jesus moment and realize what made you do it. But was your reason valid, or did you want to spare their feelings? Did you want something new? Now is the time to speak your truth.

THE EFFECTS OF CHEATING OR BEING CHEATED ON CAN HAVE SIDE EFFECTS THAT CAN LAST FOR YEARS. DO ANY OF THESE POST-CHEATING SITUATIONS SOUND FAMILIAR? ARGUING THEN HAVING STEAMY MAKE-UP SEX, FINGER-POINTING, CHECKING PHONES, SPYING AND INTERROGATING, HAVING REGRETS, AND SELF-DOUBTING. THEN IT'S BACK DOWN MEMORY LANE AND AROUND THE CYCLE GOES UNTIL ONE PERSON HAS HAD ENOUGH.

Let's be clear, it's not enough to know that it was an offensive act. You must understand you did the offense to your partner's heart and own it. Your ex had reasonable expectations that an exclusive relationship was mutual. If there was no discussion on being in an open relationship, you changed the narrative without informing your partner. How would you feel if they did that to you?

It's also not wise to pile up your emotional baggage on the other person while using manipulative tactics to get them to feel sorry for you. For example, now is not the time to cry about how much you love them! It only pleased you while you left your partner in the dark.

IT'S THE FACT THAT AT THAT VERY MOMENT, YOU DECIDED TO DO WHAT WAS ONLY BEST FOR YOU, THAT ONLY SATISFIED YOU, WHILE NOT ALLOWING YOUR PARTNER THE RIGHT TO CHOOSE THE BEST COURSE FOR THEMSELVES IN A FRAIL RELATIONSHIP.

3. Lying / Manipulation

Lying is like a temporary fix that buys you time to solve a larger problem. It's either something that has compounded or a quick fix. Either way, it sucks for the person on the receiving end. Some might say that it depends on the lie.

For example, if I ask how I look, the best reply would be, "you look great!" Please and Thank you. Then there are the other lies. The ones that grow like tree branches and go on and on. Now you have this brand new storyline that has to continue because you are locked in tight like your passwords.

If you know that you are less ambitious but more opportunistic, why are you masking your truth to mirror your partner? Eventually, the facts will reveal your character. If you ask to borrow money knowing it was their last, with no intentions to pay it back, that's just trifling. And why do you continue to keep your dating profile active?

Convenient amnesia is not an excuse. Why do you act confident but over-exaggerate everything? The best thing is to hold yourself accountable and be transparent so that no one can dispute your character later on. No one feels safe with someone who has to lie to stand tall and be accepted.

4. Insecurities

We have moments when we doubt our capabilities or value. The good news is that it gets better when you practice positive mantras, decluttering outdated beliefs and negative thoughts. In the meantime, if your self-talk sounds more like trash talk to yourself how do you think that it's going to be transmitted outwardly to others?

REMEMBER WHEN I SAID
THAT I WOULD GET TO IT
LATER ON?

I didn't expect the center of myself to be fragile when it came to relationships. At that time, I didn't know about instincts, or positive self-talk, nor possessed the emotional maturity to love someone else. I didn't grow up with my father for most of my life and later realized that I was looking for him in other men.

Before I got into a relationship, I was bubbly, confident, and ready to take over the world. Afterward, I felt like a different person. I also experienced domestic abuse, which was another layer to deal with on my journey. During that era, I attracted the wrong people who tried to dictate how much my worth was to control me.

THE BEST LESSON THAT I
DISCOVERED WAS THAT
HURT AND HEALED
PEOPLE NEVER SPEAK
THE SAME LANGUAGE AT
THE SAME TIME.

I DON'T SAY THESE THINGS TO GAIN SYMPATHY BUT TO SHOW YOU THAT YOU ARE NOT ALONE IF YOU HAVE A BROKEN PAST. THE PAST FOLLOWS US ALL UNTIL IT GETS OUR FULL ATTENTION. WHEN WE ANSWER THE CALL, IT BENEFITS EVERYONE. YOUR STORY TODAY WILL NOT BE THE SAME TOMORROW. HOWEVER, IF YOU ONLY MAKE ROOM FOR THE SAME TEMPO, YOU WILL STAY AT THE SAME LEVEL IN ANY RELATIONSHIP.

5. Lack of Affection/Attention

Nothing is drier than having a partner who shows a lack of affection and attention and lets it dwindle after they've won your heart. You used to give compliments and daily text messages of something sweet that kept the imagination and anticipation growing stronger.

But then it stopped cold. Now the drive-thru Chick-fil-A girl is getting called sweetheart, while your significant other is getting called insecure or immature.

How did we get here?

If there is no affection and no daily words or acts of love, we are sex buddies with a title. It would help if you were treating your relationship differently and better than others. If you decided they came last, then they eventually determined that you were the last.

6. Money Turnoffs/ Clashing Financial Personalities

Having mixed views about money or establishing a financially secure future makes a significant impact on a relationship. Are you a penny pincher? Or do you like to max out credit cards or gamble a paycheck away? What do you think about spending money on date nights and buying flowers?

Are you an aggressive investor, and are they a pre-investor or moderate? Or do you overshare and then expect to have control over your partner?

We can't forget about people who like to dry beg. Meaning you mention hardships and hope that you will get others to rescue you financially.

It's okay if you are a saver and they are a spender as long as you talk openly about your financial personality. Talking about finances and credit scores often is a touchy subject and usually comes up much later when the relationship has grown. If you say that you are okay with splitting 50/50 but really prefer a partner to provide 100% of everything, practice discussing expectations before misunderstandings.

7. Lack of Emotional Maturity/ Lazy Emotionally

You could be two hard-working people and very successful in your lanes. Yet, just like a lazy person, you sweep emotions under the rug when it comes to the bond. You leave the dust of disagreements lurking around, and like dirty dishes piled up in the sink, so are your most authentic feelings waiting tirelessly on a call to action.

Eventually, the truth comes to the surface, and by that time, it's one big mess. No one wants to compromise unless the other person goes first. It's all talking, but no one is actively listening to what the other person is saying. You profess your love but have no idea how to love them or yourself.

Nevertheless, you rather be with them than be with no one has been your winning strategy. To you, a self-care concept means abstaining from having sex for two months or dating new people while holding your emotions like a clenched fist. Just because you take care of your responsibilities, like paying your bills on time and keeping a roof over your head, doesn't mean that you can handle emotional maturity.

8. Addictions

Another trigger to break up is addictions. Some addictions on the lighter side are cleaning, working, and exercising. On the other hand, more challenging things to shake are drugs, alcohol, attention-seeking, etc. When I think of addictions, I think of a safe space that one creates to cope with deeper-seeded feelings that we desire to numb.

Compulsive behaviors are distractions that give us something that no one else can provide. It's the green light that we give ourselves to avoid making any change. Being addicted to something or someone is usually intense and gives us an incredible rush with instantaneous results. It doesn't matter who we hurt as long as we're not the ones that feel it. It's all about getting our cravings met.

Concerning having a partner, this doesn't just affect you but them as well. They know your patterns, reactions, and unwillingness to bend. Getting you to admit that you have a problem can turn into a battle. Addictions can also be the ones that we consider "other problems."

You over-talk, worry excessively, and get fiery mad, and defensive. You like drama more than happiness, and so forth. You don't need a high to feel satisfaction. It just takes setting boundaries and facing what you're feeling instead of reacting or looking for an escape.

9. Family/Friends Influence

Our safe space usually involves people that are closest to us. Our family and friends are the ones that know about the beginning of new love, the breaking points, and the end. Sometimes, they know too much for our relationship to survive or have a fair chance of becoming successful.

Let's face it, not every person comes in a perfect package, and that can be terrifying for loved ones to witness.
Instead of being a relationship between two people, it has turned into a reality show for all eyes to see.
Because once other people's opinions seep in, it just opens the door for doubts to grow bigger while confidence fades away.
Then the circus begins, and unfavorable remarks get duly noted.

I get it. Sometimes we need wise counsel. Nevertheless, it gets dicey when you enable others to dictate your every move and give opinions about someone they know nothing about firsthand. When you start off letting other people lead your relationship, you are welcoming everything and anything that could potentially cloud your judgment when you could have trusted your intuition.

However, if there is a case of someone getting mistreated, or abused in any way, including verbal, emotional, physical, financial, or spiritual, your loved ones have every cause to worry about your safety or part in the violation.

10. You still have old baggage from former relationships

It's funny how you can be in a brand new relationship, and it feels like you're merely continuing where you left off from the last one. This approach might seem like it's not a big deal, but it will show the consequences later on.

When the misunderstandings begin, things get a little more heated. Then hurtful words get thrown around that could never be taken back.

The insults fly, and the subliminal texts drop ever so passive-aggressively with the right amount of sting. Or, power plays like disappearing acts or 24hr breakups to regain control commences.

You could have avoided all of these antics if you gave yourself time to heal and reflect. Now it's a new relationship, and it's filled with comparisons, old habits, and missed opportunities.

If you want to increase your chances with a new bond, it's time to get rid of old baggage like self-sabotaging patterns, prideful ways, and the memories of your past relationship.

NOW HOW DO WE FIX
IT?

GET THE PERSON BACK?

How about we get you back?

Let's face it. It took a lot of repetitive patterns for you to get here at this point. Going back to the relationship or trying to get them back is not going to make things better. It will only give you comfort - at best. But what price are you willing to pay for it?

Better question, why would you? As a woman who has dealt with men that were not respecting the split, I thought it was important to offer tools that would help others understand the consequences of actions and the importance of respecting someone's wishes to end the relationship.

You could be saying, Lesley, I wasn't that kind of person. I didn't act that way. Maybe you didn't exactly, but this is not about crucifying you or saying that you are less than if you did. It's about helping someone who wishes to be done with their negative ways or struggles and heal from a breakup.

There are many reasons why a connection comes to an end. Yet, they all tend to fall under the most relatable reasons for many people. Even if you are the sweetest, kindest person who can't catch a break, this is also for you! I got tired of seeing in the news about people not accepting breakups and going overboard or struggling to get over one.

No matter where you are on the scale, these tips will help you in the bigger picture of healing.

You know what you
did and didn't do or
could have done more
to save the
relationship.
Hindsight tells the
truth. Your ex
decided that the best
thing was to be
friends or part ways
for good. It is their
wish, and it must be
acknowledged even if
you disagree.

Depending on the relationship, maybe it was timing, financial, or wanting something new. Perhaps it was a lack of affection or attention, and it became too late to fix it. Now is the time for the next step of your life.

— — —

How to heal from a breakup.

1. Honor their wish to be friends.

When someone breaks up with you, it's hard to believe it. Going from an intimate to a platonic situation never feels like an easy thing to do. At the moment, you have to stomach hearing the news of the ending of your connection. Sometimes you didn't see it coming. Even if you had clues, you figured things were not that bad.

Still, the choice has been made to no longer be together anymore. We ask ourselves, "What did I do?" Don't make it harder or more complicated than it has to be. If you need time to get your emotions together, don't ask why if you know that you can't handle it.

You already had an idea deep down because there were signs, withdrawals, and talks long before your ex made this choice. You will make it more challenging if you give them the power to provide you with closure. You have enough inner strength to say Thanks, Good Luck, and to let it go.

2. Please don't ask to call them or to meet up.

Asking to meet up and see each other is not suitable for you or the other person shortly after the split. Some people break up to make up. Still, this is not that moment. The message is clear and should be accepted.

The same thing goes for contacting them periodically yet methodically.

If you know the relationship ended, especially if on bad terms, there should be no reason to speak or clear the air any longer. If you are holding out for getting physical touch with hopes that it will make a difference, this is also a selfish act that benefits you.

You know what turns them on, what makes them smile, and trying to reignite your physical attraction will still bring you back to the problems and the end result.

3. Stop giving them daily updates or sharing highs and lows in your life.

The more you try to guilt-trip a continuation of the relationship, the worse the results will be in the long run. Not to mention, their respect for you will dwindle. When you first met, it was all hot and steamy and unlike anything before.

Now, it's "oh, it's you" vibes with lukewarm humidifier streams.

Give people time to decide how they want to move forward with you in their life, and that could take weeks, months, years, or never! You can't push onto others your frustrations with the decision and expect things to go your way. Any relationship must be a freedom of choice, not an obligation.

By the way, where was this energy before?

Why are you trying so hard now? Is it because you don't want them to be with someone else? Does it drive you crazy? These are not reasons to be with someone for the long term. These are reasons to take control. If you love them, you would also have respect for them and their choices. Most importantly, you would have respect for yourself.

4. Change your number or block theirs and unfollow them on social media.

Things have changed after you both decided to be more than friends, but now you are no longer together. And if you want to heal, you have to cut out all communication. If you had a hard time with the breakup, it's just going to be too tempting to dial them up once in a while.

Reaching out to your ex might seem harmless, but we both know that you have an ulterior motive. You're trying to assess the call to see if your former flame still loves you or, in a new relationship, happier, and that's a no, no! No one needs to be interrupted abruptly in their life by you with your "CHECKING IN" ploys, especially when they have started healing and moving on in their life.

The same goes for following each other on social media. Remove their pictures and unfollow them. Block them if need be. If you are trying to heal from the pain, you must stop the pain's bleeding or source. It does no good for you if you are always watching them live on without you. Also, if you are a competitive person, this would only tempt you to compete! Now, you are creating a nonverbal dialogue that stems from your head and not in reality.

5. Do not live in memory lane.

I can't tell you how many people do this and think it's okay. I probably stayed longer in a relationship with one guy because he would always sing me the memory lane song, and I would melt every time I revisited old memories until it no longer worked. It's one thing to reflect on what happened and think about the lessons learned.

It's another thing to play repeatedly, the good and bad times over and over in your head.

Then, you take it up another notch and play out new scenarios as if the person is there. They are not! They are not in your head talking back to you. The scenes then remind you of a specific song, event, or secrets you shared, etc. By doing this practice, it will only deter your growth and ability to make a clean break.

6. Please don't make a friend request or create a fake account.

Have you ever heard the saying love them from a distance? That couldn't be more prevalent in this case. Unless you have kids or a shared business, you no longer have a reason to be in their life. Following them on social media is no exception. Even if Facebook suggests that you might know the person, click ignore.

It is a new phase, and if you don't get focused and stay on track, you run the risk of dwelling in a sinking ship that will go down with only you in it.

There is no need to make a friend request or create a fake account to keep tabs on them. Nor do you need to use people to leak information or carry information back to your ex. Speaking of using people, please do not flirt with their friends as bait to get them back.

I AM A TRUE BELIEVER IN
DESTINY, AND THAT MEANS
THAT PIECES WILL FALL
WHERE THEY NEED TO - IF
MEANT TO BE.

SOMETIMES THE UNIVERSE
USES PEOPLE TO HELP
MOTIVATE YOU TO STEP
INTO ANOTHER LEVEL
WITHIN YOUR LIFE. MAYBE
YOUR EX REPRESENTED
CHARACTERISTICS OF YOU
THAT NEED ATTENTION OR
GROOMING. LISTEN TO THE
SIGNS WITHOUT FORCING A
PREFERRED NARRATIVE
INSTEAD. IF YOU GIVE IT
TIME, BETTER DAYS WILL BE
ON THE WAY.

7. Do not contact them for the holidays or their birthday.

.

I thought this was an important step to help move on after a breakup. You might think that it would be okay to contact your ex-sweetheart because it's a joyful time of the year. I say resist this temptation at all costs. Especially if you broke up around the holidays, it's a big no-no.

Here's why there is too much emotional attachment to that time, and if you've never cleared the air about the issues, it will remind you of what went wrong, when, how, and with whom. Not to mention, they could be seeing someone else already, and it would make things awkward if they get a call or text from you. Maybe your ex contacts you first. It's okay to reply but keep it short! Follow their lead and listen to what is said and **NOT** said.

After all, they could still care about you and just want to make sure that you are okay. Plus, if your ex is interested, you will know. How would you know if your ex is interested? Your love interest will say it in many ways! They might flat out say it, or they might bring up old romantic times, like when you first kissed. They'll want to know if you're seeing anyone and offer their availability to talk more.

I'M ONLY GIVING THESE
SUGGESTIVE TIPS BUT
NOT ADVISING YOU TO
LOOK FOR IT OR WORK
FOR IT. THESE EXAMPLES
ARE HYPOTHETICAL AND
DEPEND ON THE
TEMPERATURE OF THE
RELATIONSHIP.

8. Do not try to minimize or twist your ex's words about the breakup.

Let's say that you have some contact with them because of work, where you live, etc. The absolute last thing that you want to do is minimize or twist your ex's words. Whether right or wrong, the decision is best for them, and we must focus on this decision. There has to be a time in your life for accountability.

It does not mean that you are a monster. At a minimum, it means something that your former partner did not get and was not happy enough to continue in the relationship. Now at this very moment, you have an opportunity to reevaluate yourself. It might just surprise you!

Maybe you pursue someone for looks and not substance. Perhaps it was a power move that you both benefited from at the time. Or, you were lonely and just wanted your former mate there rather than being alone with unresolved feelings. Who you were at that moment attracted a person who had a message for your life.

The question is, can you move away from the experience of the breakup, look within to get the reason you needed them, and they needed you?

9. Please don't call them for validation.

The problem with getting over a breakup is often the temptation to try to get them back. Unfortunately, that notion overtakes thinking things out clearly at times. So what do you do? You had a terrible day or were feeling low and remembered how that person would comfort you, and you needed their validation or affirmations.

If you could hear them say that things will be okay and ask about you and your family or what happened with that situation, this would cheer you up. Have you considered what this will do for them? You see, when you have an intimate relationship with someone, and it goes sour, you don't get to pick and choose what remains.

You don't get to contact them and get their affection in the way that they used to do for you. They're not calling you babe, sweetheart, or rubbing your back, or giving you tight hugs anymore. By expecting this old treatment, you will be setting yourself up for a huge disappointment.

Instead of understanding they moved on, you will take it as a slight, or they've changed and not the sweet, loving, kind person that you once knew. Now they're mean, cold, and detached. When in reality, their feelings have changed for you.

10. Do not play sad music.

Isn't this a sad time? Yes! But it could be freeing, too, if you weigh the pros and cons. Music is excellent, and I love listening to it and setting up playlists for my desired mood. If I want to workout, I will play the music that gets me excited to move fast.

If I want to do yoga or have downtime, I will play something tranquil for the mood to slow down. If I am going through a breakup, I'm playing music to pick me up! I am not lighting a match to make flames. Break up tunes are fantastic, but it can guide your thoughts to deeper, angrier, or sadder feelings than it has to be.

I would go a step further and focus on the lyrics of the song. It can dampen your mood and draw a picture that is too vivid. Why not play something happy? Something about survival, faith, and being independent and elevating?

Do you really need to listen to a song that will make you drunk dial and do something that you would regret? I hope the answer is no. Take it from me; when that high comes back down, you want to have your dignity intact. There are some things in life that you can't take back, and if you can't afford to lose it, don't gamble it away.

11. Please get rid of their stuff.

If you want to get over the breakup, you have to part with their belongings and help. Departing from their belongings includes gifts, vehicles, pictures, hats, t-shirts, hoodies, etc. This includes storing them in your spare room, basement, garage, or wherever it is easily accessible.

IT DOES NO GOOD
KNOWING THAT YOU CAN
GO BACK AND PEEK
THROUGH IT WHENEVER
YOU WANT. THESE
BELONGINGS ARE TOO
TEMPTING TO LOOK AT
AND GIVE LIFE TO THEM
AGAIN. YOUR HEART HAS
ALREADY BEEN THROUGH
A LOT, AND SO HAS YOUR
MIND'S DEFENSES
REGARDING FUTURE
RELATIONSHIPS.

Right now, you're making up new rules and setting up new boundaries for the next person to follow after your ex. They are already getting set up to fail, but so are you if you don't let go completely. If you can not do it, keep it far away and promise yourself only to return when you get healed.

Even if you received financial help from your former love, any dependency would keep the door cracked open to a messy break.

It is part of your journey, and you did spend significant time with this person. However, you have no idea how far they have already moved on, and you can't spend time trying to compare or keep any traces of them or their progress in their new life - that is without you. The goal is to heal, not to heal, and then go right back to being hurt. Let's break the cycle!

12. Don't keep feelings in your head. Write it down.

If you are trying to get over a breakup, I would advise you to journal instead of healing through it with a friend. The truth is, we all have our problems, and some friends are more judgemental or ill-prepared or preoccupied to truly meet your needs.

What if you have a moment and want to call them up at night before you drink your sorrows away or give in to temptations to call your ex, and they don't pick up? Then what?

This is not about saying that you have terrible friends; it's about learning to depend more on yourself and be more self-reliant. This is a win-win for everyone because no one will feel like they have been emotionally blackmailed or relied upon to help you grow.

Enjoy your loved ones without assigning them your newest burden. This is the time to stretch yourself and not go back to your usual way of handling things. Remember, it's all about

GETTING NEW RESULTS!

When you journal your feelings versus saying or keeping them in your head, the situation sounds much different. You might see the way that you express yourself clearer or darker when you put it on paper. There is no rule of how much has to be written down. It's about telling the truth about your feelings and getting to a happy place.

By writing your feelings down, you can go back to the older entry and see how far you've grown. Right now, it seems unimaginable that things will feel good again. Go inwardly in a healthy way, and I can promise you, it will feel even better sooner than you think.

13. Don't tell social media your breakup story.

Keep things light-hearted by only updating your single status. You might also want to keep it private to give you time. Even if the other person decides to trash you, don't take it personally. I know that it's easier said than done, but it can be done!

When you take their actions or words personally, it will feel like being trapped in a spider web. Disconnect yourself from the situation and resist giving into playing games. If you find that it might be too tempting to leave subliminal messages, then give yourself a break from social media. If you use social media as a platform for your business, automate your posts and keep your page drama-free.

Do.

If you're going to stop making these habits thrive or avoid temptation, there will be new actions or patterns that have to take place. If you quit cold turkey, then eventually, you will crave the same thing. So how do we get to this new place of breakthrough? We change the narrative.

1. Date yourself.

Who are you? What are your non-negotiables in love? Are you a compassionate person? Are you a taker and less of a giver? What do you like to do to unwind? What are some of your passions? We often know more or think we do about a person we are dating and not enough about ourselves. Or, we didn't even care to ask more questions about our former flames, and they kept notes.

We know who we are attracted to and the type of person that we would like to date. But what is attractive about you to date you? It's crucial to see what the world sees. You might think that you come across successfully in the image that you display. Yet, in reality, it is different.

By dating yourself, you give yourself time to reflect and get to know yourself better. Doesn't it sometimes feel like a stopwatch goes off the moment you start dating someone new? Once it starts, that's it. Your partner sees who you are through their eyes at that moment and during the relationship.

But what if you needed more time? Suppose you are still struggling to get over someone or find yourself? What if you can't even see your ex walking down the street? Be honest and patient with yourself. No one expects you to be perfect, but they will expect you to be fully present in this new connection.

By allowing yourself time to date yourself, you will be more confident in who you are; therefore, attracting someone who matches you in a complementary way and where you are in life.

2. Do checkups.

Now is the time to do checkups and see where your health is mentally, spiritually, physically, and financially. Let's do a quick checkup; were you compensating and paying for their love? Did you feel drained having the same conversations and playing the blame game?

On a scale of 1 - 10, how stressed are you over this breakup? Whatever is happening on the outside is directly affecting you internally.

3. Start a new regimen to relax.

Find out what calms you and create a new regime to relax. If not, it can make bad habits worse. By not setting boundaries, you can develop new addictions, and your well-being will pay for it. Try some essential oils like citrus scents and lavender, sage, or a deep scent like sandalwood and mix them up in an oil diffuser and relax.

You can also try
drinking a glass of
warm water with lemon
and honey, and you will
feel instantly calm and
centered.

4. Practice Breathing Exercises and Meditation.

It's necessary to practice breathing and meditation to increase your chances of a breakthrough. You can count down 10 - 1 inhale, then exhale. This tactic is super easy and gives instant results. Having healing practices in place helps you be calm and keep things in a better perspective. Think of it like brakes to a car. You got this!

5. Say out loud 10 things that you are grateful for.

Think about what you're grateful for in your life, then say it or write it down. I personally like to write it down because it allows me to revisit and reflect. By focusing on what you are thankful for, you increase your chances of being happy and less focused on the thoughts that bring you down.

When we take a moment to think about what we appreciate, we move away from thinking about what we lost. After all, you are still here, and there is so much more to learn and experience.

Imagine if you looked at life from this perspective more; where do you think you would be? Give yourself a chance to be present instead of focusing on what's ahead or has already passed.

6. Focus on your personal goals or aspirations.

What did you always want to try but never made the time to do it? Is it updating your look? How about getting a piercing or tattoo? Would you like to learn to cook new meals or try a new career? Is there a degree that you would like to attain?

Or, is there somewhere you wanted to visit and add a stamp to your passport? Anything that moves you forward, touches your heart, and puts a smile on your face deserves your attention now! At this moment, this is the time to better yourself and make no apologies about it.

7. Forgive yourself.

The first thing that we often do is wonder what we did wrong after a breakup. We start playing scenarios in our heads, looking for clues that led to the end of the road. Some of us go for the jugular and blame ourselves, hurt ourselves, and declare that we will never move on. It's tough because you don't get that person to console you.

Your ex hurt you, or you hurt them, but you still want them to fix it. You yearn for your ex to address it until your soul gets patched back up. It can't be both ways. The best thing that you can do is to forgive yourself and them. What does forgiving have to do with this?

Everything. It's the signage that leads to freedom of the pain. You let go of the events, hurtful words, memories, fuzzy feelings, happier times, and the blame game.

8. Take ownership.

You might be at a place where you feel horrible and want to take responsibility. Here is the difference to help you know how to do it.

The difference with taking ownership is that ownership makes the responsible decision to correct a wrong, admit the wrong, and commit to keeping it right moving forward. It is not based on popularity but purpose.

Blaming yourself is like a wildfire of blame, pain, and self-sabotage. You acknowledge your part, but you make yourself suffer mercilessly. This brings us back to why forgiving ourselves is crucial. Forgiving yourself is being compassionate to yourself. You let go of their memories, actions, and kisses and stop the idealization of the what-ifs. This will clear your path to move ahead free of guilt or shame.

9. Find and protect your happy place.

This place is sacred. It's in your heart and mind and gives you a smile in your spirit **that no one can break.** Please make no mistake; it takes work to get there, but it will be worth it. We spend so much time looking for our soulmate in relationships, work, and social status in life when nothing can replace the peace within.

When you have not found it, you will search tirelessly. At times, you might collect multiple relationships together to improve your chances. Chances are, it will not be successful in trying to use a cheat sheet to acquire peace. It is a walk by one to find one.

10. Set yourself up for success.

I am a firm believer in taking a loss and turning it into a win. Everything you have experienced has brought you a golden lesson. Yet, it will only reveal the teaching if you accept accountability. If you see your temporary loss as a failure of self, you will feel like the world blames you.

If you pull the reins in and look at it from a self-aware perspective, you will have a much easier time because you're open to learning, improving, and elevating.

11. Understand and believe that no love can not find you.

Who you are and what you want will always be within your reach. The slow down or delay is not to hurt you but to lift you higher! Why waste another second obsessing over something or someone when there is a better situation around the corner?

Growing shouldn't feel like torture. Instead, if you choose to see it as a gift for you to gather, learn and elevate, you will be where you want to be sooner than later. It is not rejection. It is not ready. When the time is right, you will be amazed at who you become and who you attract.

12. Learn so you don't repeat history.

If you stay at the level of reminiscing over someone who hurt you and got away with it, then you will keep playing the same song and most likely get the same results in the future. Why? Because you didn't learn. You can't stop feeling or visualizing the betrayal of your heart getting broken.

By resisting, in a sense, you are choosing to walk the path of protesting the pain that someone caused you, rather than owning the parts you played to receive the pain. Forget about who wins and loses.

Growth rules over everything!

13. Reflect on your progress.

Now is the time to look at some of the new actions taken and see how far you've come. Keep yourself on the hook for your efforts and be in good spirits with these new habits. Look yourself in the mirror and smile! Laugh more or simply be still. Take 20 minutes or however long and schedule alone time to think about how far you have come.

REAL PROGRESS IS IN THE
BABY STEPS. EVERY TIME
YOU REACH A NEW PHASE,
YOU SHOULD BE PROUD.

**YOU ARE FREE TO CHANGE
YOUR MIND.**

MAYBE YOU HAD YOUR
PLANS SET ON BEING WITH
A SPECIFIC PERSON OR
COULD NEVER SEE
YOURSELF WITH SOMEONE
YOUR FAMILY DISAPPROVES
OF. AS LONG AS YOU HAVE
BREATH, YOU ARE FREE TO
GROW, AND THAT
INCLUDES CHANGING YOUR
MIND. DON'T LET SOCIETY,
OLD BELIEFS, OR FEAR
DICTATE WHAT PATH YOU
ARE SET ON.

By listening to your
intuition and
following your heart,
you will always be led
in the best direction,
even if it looks
different.

It's all about growth.

Let's assume that you are ready for growth over everything. Now is the time to tap into the person that you were on your way to becoming. Nothing has changed with your destiny. You just got distracted by a small part of it.

You know who you are. Your love isn't puffed up, it's real, and someone would be crazy to walk away from the new you (don't tell them that, by the way). You have so much to offer, and you require the same energy in return.

Who can resist the new you?

The goal is not about becoming a perfect person, nor tell you that you will never experience heartache again. Love requires taking a chance, and chances are, you will cry again. Hopefully, it will bring less pain and more tears of joy instead.

A PARTNER NEEDS THE
SAME THINGS YOU NEED.
THEY NEED THE REAL YOU
TO SHOW UP. THEY NEED
TO SEE YOUR
VULNERABILITIES AND NOT
BE USED AS A PUNCHING
BAG WHEN LIFE GETS
TOUGH. THEY ARE HUMAN
AND CAN ONLY TAKE SO
MUCH - LIKE YOU. ALL YOU
NEED TO DO IS REDEFINE
WHAT LOVE MEANS TO
YOUR HEART, AND YOU
WILL FIND YOUR WAY.

JUST DON'T TAKE SOMEONE FOR A RIDE IF YOU ARE NOT 100% READY.

FURTHERMORE, BE CAREFUL WHO YOUR LOVE IDOL IS. ARE YOU USING TV, SOCIAL MEDIA, OR HOW YOU SAW YOUR PARENTS' LOVE AS YOUR GUIDANCE? THE TIME IS NOW TO SET A NEW TREND THAT IS ALL ABOUT YOU AND NO LONGER IN SOMEONE ELSE'S SHADOW. TRUST YOUR LOVE LANGUAGE.

How will I know when I
have a breakthrough?

A breakthrough isn't a person but a destination. It is the unshakable peace that once you find it, you keep with you. You might discount its power because it is not loud. Nor does it give you robust results in plain sight. It's not supposed to do that. Peace is within. It is the result of self-work and builds on your self-worth.

No love can evade you when all of the stars align. If it does, that means that it is not your star.

They said what?

There seems to be a disconnect in society with acceptance. If it's not a happy ending, then it's a terrible situation. If you don't win, it makes you a loser. When your ex didn't choose you, that means that you are not worthy. My question is, who lied to you, and why did you believe it?

Destiny is destiny. It doesn't mean that destiny always appears in a winning situation. The most significant wins come in our most incredible times of losing. What might seem like a dark time can also be the Universe grabbing your attention to elevate you.

Closing

It's time to celebrate and make room for a better you and a new relationship that you will attract. The best thing is to focus on yourself, learn from the past, and commit to integrity, yielding better results in the future. At times, it might feel lonely not having them there anymore. However, nothing is worse than holding up another person's heart as a backup plan until you get over your ex or issues. It's emotional extortion and not fair to other people or you.

Make a clean break and seek wise counsel when necessary, and always trust your gut. When you focus on improving yourself and prioritize things that make you happy, you will be amazed at the people you will attract. After all, you can't force someone to erase their negative impression of you, and you will waste time trying. If you do cross paths, let it be organically and not strategically.

And please don't try one last attempt to tie anyone down with long-term commitments like a baby, pets, property, an engagement, or threatening to do harm to yourself. These ideas often have disastrous outcomes (minus a child's blessing) if the motive is out of fear of losing control.

Good news is coming...

I HOPE YOU FEEL A WEIGHT HAS LIFTED OFF OF YOU AND YOU BEGIN TO SEE THIS NEW CHAPTER AS A GOOD THING. THE UNIVERSE WILL KNOW IF YOU TRY TO DOUBLE-DIP AND PLAY BOTH SIDES BECAUSE IT WILL SHOW UP IN YOUR LIFE IN REAL TIME. DON'T LET YOUR PRIDE LEAD YOU DOWN A PATH THAT WILL ONLY HAVE PAIN WAITING FOR YOU.

Reward yourself with a fresh start and a new break from a place that no longer feeds your heart and soul. Only you have the power to do it! Your partner is not there to do the work that must be done solely by you. They have to be whole and, therefore, will love you better when you don't demand it.

Time well spent

Use this time to get closer to spiritual love, and you will find that everything will make more sense. Listen to your feelings moving forward, and always remember to do breathing exercises to control your emotions. Be grateful for the little things, and bigger things will flourish as you truly wish. Always stay present and never forget this moment or what you've learned from the breakup, aka breakthrough!

How long before the pain goes away?

Oh yeah, how long will it take to heal from a breakup? It depends on how much life you keep breathing into it. Have you ever decided to forgive someone, and the hurt was still there, but then, one day, you didn't feel it anymore? The same method can work for healing from a breakup. Keep sending them well wishes whenever they cross your mind and set the energy free.

Be respectful to the energy and say only good things. These practices will feel awkward and make no sense to other people. So it's probably best to keep it to yourself. Keep wishing them well and picture yourself happy, healed, and in a long-lasting relationship. Picture it, and let it come to you in your mind organically.

Never try to force a manifestation.

By the time you put all of these tips together, it will feel like you never lost any time but gained an untapped better part of yourself.

May you honor this moment in your life and commit to moving forward in perfect peace.

Love and light,
Lesley

LESLEY D. NURSE

WWW.LESLEYNURSE.COM

Break Free and Create Your Dream Life

Lesley is a dynamic force dedicated to empowering individuals to break free from the shackles of their own limitations and unlock their true potential. With a burning passion for helping others, Lesley has made it her life's mission for people to create the life they desire.

With her captivating books and numerous other pursuits, Lesley invites you to embark on a transformative journey of self-discovery and personal growth. Her words resonate with authenticity, wisdom, and a deep understanding of the human experience.

YOU ARE IN COMPLETE
CONTROL OF DESIGNING
YOUR LIFE.
COLOR IT JOYFULLY & BRAVELY.

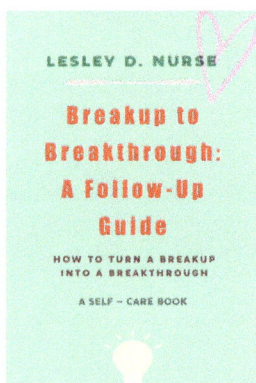

LESLEY D. NURSE

**Breakup to
Breakthrough:
A Follow-Up
Guide**

HOW TO TURN A BREAKUP
INTO A BREAKTHROUGH

A SELF – CARE BOOK

WHEN GOING THROUGH A BREAKUP, IT'S CRUCIAL TO FOCUS ON BOOSTING YOUR SELF-ASSURANCE AND INNER STRENGTH. THE "BREAKUP TO BREAKTHROUGH: A FOLLOW-UP GUIDE" WORKBOOK IS AN INVALUABLE RESOURCE THAT CAN HELP YOU ACCOMPLISH THIS GOAL. THIS GUIDE PROVIDES PRACTICAL ADVICE FOR ALLEVIATING EMOTIONAL DISTRESS AND GUIDING YOU TOWARDS PERSONAL GROWTH AND SELF-EXPLORATION. WITH JOURNALING PROMPTS, COLORING PAGES, AND MOTIVATIONAL QUOTES, IT OFFERS PEACE AND ASSISTANCE IN ATTAINING LIBERATION. THIS GUIDE IS A MUST-HAVE FOR ANYONE EXPERIENCING A BREAKUP.

It is always possible to redefine who you are and to own it.

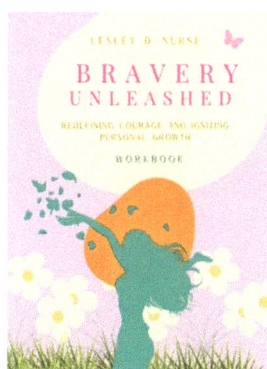

If you're in need of a quick confidence boost, the **Bravery Unleashed: Redefining Courage and Igniting Personal Growth** workbook may be just what you need. It's designed to help you unlock your true potential in a supportive environment, break free from negative thoughts, and unleash your inner bravery. Remember, life can be challenging, but this guide will aid you in getting back on track and conquering any obstacle in your path.

YOUR BREAKTHROUGH STARTS NOW...

Unblock Your Joy

HAVING CLEAR OBJECTIVES CAN LEAD TO
UNEXPECTED ACHIEVEMENTS. IT'S CRUCIAL TO
ENSURE YOUR GOALS ALIGN WITH YOUR DEEPEST
DESIRES, AND YOU'RE FREE TO HAVE AS MANY
OBJECTIVES AS YOU WANT.

DATES :   MOOD :

GOAL   TO DO LIST

Daily Journal

DATES :   **MOOD :**

before I dated them, I was...

_____

_____

_____

_____

_____

_____

_____

before J dated them, J was...

before I dated them, I was...

before I dated them, I was...

before I dated them, I was...

before I dated them, I was...

BREAKTHROUGH

Daily Journal

DATES :   **MOOD :**

while I dated them, I was...

_____

_____

_____

_____

_____

_____

_____

_____

while I dated them, I was...

while I dated them, I was...

while I dated them, I was...

while I dated them, I was...

while I dated them, I was...

Daily Journal

DATES :   **MOOD :**

after I dated them, I was...

_____

_____

_____

_____

_____

_____

_____

after I dated them, I was...

after I dated them, I was...

after I dated them, I was...

after I dated them, I was...

after I dated them, I was...

BREAKTHROUGH

Daily Journal

DATES :   **MOOD :**

before I dated them, I was...

_____

_____

_____

_____

_____

_____

_____

before I dated them, I was...

before I dated them, I was...

before I dated them, I was...

before I dated them, I was...

before I dated them, I was...

Daily Journal

DATES :   **MOOD :**

while I dated them, I was...

_____

_____

_____

_____

_____

_____

_____

while I dated them, I was...

while I dated them, I was...

while I dated them, I was...

while I dated them, I was...

while I dated them, I was...

Daily Journal

DATES :   **MOOD :**

after I dated them, I was...

_____

_____

_____

_____

_____

_____

_____

after I dated them, I was...

after I dated them, I was...

after I dated them, I was...

after I dated them, I was...

after I dated them, I was...

Daily Journal

DATES :   **MOOD :**

before I dated them, I was...

_____

_____

_____

_____

_____

_____

_____

_____

before I dated them, I was...

before I dated them, I was...

_____
_____
_____
_____
_____
_____
_____
_____
_____
_____
_____
_____
_____
_____
_____

before I dated them, I was...

before I dated them, I was...

before I dated them, I was...

BREAKTHROUGH

Daily Journal

DATES :   **MOOD :**

while J dated them, J was...

_____

_____

_____

_____

_____

_____

_____

_____

while I dated them, I was...

while I dated them, I was...

while I dated them, I was...

while I dated them, I was...

while I dated them, I was...

Daily Journal

DATES :   **MOOD :**

after I dated them, I was...

_____

_____

_____

_____

_____

_____

_____

after I dated them, I was...

after I dated them, I was...

after I dated them, I was...

after I dated them, I was...

after I dated them, I was...

BREAKTHROUGH

Daily Journal

DATES :   **MOOD :**

today, I Am...

today, I Am...

today, I Am...

today, I Am...

today, I Am...

_____
_____
_____
_____
_____
_____
_____
_____
_____
_____
_____
_____
_____
_____
_____
_____
_____
_____
_____
_____

today, I Am...

www.ingramcontent.com/pod-product-compliance
Lightning Source LLC
Chambersburg PA
CBHW052112030426
42335CB00025B/2944